50 Premium Secret Meal Dishes

By: Kelly Johnson

Table of Contents

- Truffle-Infused Wagyu Steak
- Black Garlic Butter Lobster Tail
- Foie Gras-Stuffed Quail
- 24K Gold Leaf Kobe Beef Sliders
- Caviar and Champagne Risotto
- Saffron-Infused Seafood Paella
- Smoked Duck Breast with Cherry Reduction
- Hand-Rolled Uni Sushi with Shiso
- Bone Marrow and Truffle Ravioli
- A5 Wagyu Tartare with Quail Egg
- Lobster Thermidor with Cognac Sauce
- Charcoal-Grilled Tomahawk Steak
- Black Truffle and Parmesan Gnocchi
- Miso-Glazed Black Cod
- Oxtail Consommé with Wild Mushrooms
- Szechuan Peppercorn-Crusted Lamb Chops
- 48-Hour Braised Short Ribs
- Peking Duck with Caviar Pancakes
- Alaskan King Crab in Garlic Butter Sauce
- Handmade Burrata with Aged Balsamic
- Black Truffle and Lobster Mac & Cheese
- Japanese A5 Wagyu Sukiyaki
- Saffron and Champagne Butter Scallops
- Dry-Aged Ribeye with Smoked Salt
- Caramelized Miso Chilean Sea Bass
- Bluefin Tuna Tataki with Ponzu Foam
- Fire-Grilled Iberico Pork Chops
- Roasted Bone Marrow with Truffle Crostini
- 24-Hour Slow-Smoked Brisket
- Lobster and Caviar Eggs Benedict
- Duck Confit with Blackberry Glaze
- Sous Vide Filet Mignon with Bordelaise
- Foie Gras-Topped Wagyu Burger
- Wild Mushroom and White Wine Risotto
- Périgord Truffle Omelette

- Honey-Glazed Roasted Poussin
- Braised Venison with Red Wine Reduction
- Saffron-Butter Poached Langoustines
- Uni Carbonara with Freshly Cracked Pepper
- Blackened Mahi-Mahi with Pineapple Salsa
- Lobster Bisque with Cognac Cream
- Aged Parmesan and Black Truffle Fondue
- Charcoal-Grilled Mediterranean Octopus
- Porcini-Dusted Veal Chop
- Yuzu-Marinated Hamachi Crudo
- Spiced Moroccan Lamb Tagine
- 24-Hour Slow-Braised Pork Belly
- Sea Urchin and Bottarga Pasta
- Espresso-Rubbed Prime Rib
- Miso Caramelized Scallops with Sake Reduction

Truffle-Infused Wagyu Steak

Ingredients:

- 2 A5 Wagyu ribeye steaks
- 1 tbsp black truffle oil
- 1 tbsp unsalted butter
- 1 tsp sea salt
- ½ tsp freshly cracked black pepper
- Fresh black truffle (for shaving)

Instructions:

1. Let Wagyu steaks sit at room temperature for 30 minutes.
2. Heat a cast-iron skillet over medium-high heat.
3. Brush steaks with truffle oil, then season with salt and pepper.
4. Sear each side for 1-2 minutes for a perfect medium-rare crust.
5. Add butter and baste the steak for extra richness.
6. Remove from heat, let rest for 5 minutes, and shave fresh truffle on top before serving.

Black Garlic Butter Lobster Tail

Ingredients:

- 2 lobster tails
- 2 tbsp black garlic butter (mashed black garlic mixed with butter)
- 1 tbsp lemon juice
- ½ tsp smoked paprika
- ½ tsp sea salt
- 1 tbsp chopped parsley

Instructions:

1. Preheat the oven to 400°F (200°C).
2. Cut the lobster shells down the center and pull the meat slightly out.
3. Mix black garlic butter, lemon juice, smoked paprika, and salt.
4. Spread the butter over the lobster meat.
5. Bake for 12-15 minutes until the lobster is opaque and tender.
6. Garnish with parsley before serving.

Foie Gras-Stuffed Quail

Ingredients:

- 2 whole quails, cleaned
- 3 oz foie gras, diced
- ½ cup brioche crumbs
- 1 tbsp truffle oil
- 1 tbsp cognac
- ½ tsp salt
- ½ tsp black pepper

Instructions:

1. Preheat the oven to 375°F (190°C).
2. Mix foie gras, brioche crumbs, truffle oil, and cognac to make the stuffing.
3. Stuff the quails and season with salt and pepper.
4. Roast for 20-25 minutes until golden brown and cooked through.
5. Serve with a rich port wine reduction.

24K Gold Leaf Kobe Beef Sliders

Ingredients:

- ½ lb Kobe beef, ground
- 2 brioche slider buns
- 2 slices aged cheddar cheese
- 1 tbsp truffle aioli
- 2 small gold leaf sheets
- ½ tsp salt
- ½ tsp black pepper

Instructions:

1. Form Kobe beef into small patties and season with salt and pepper.
2. Cook in a skillet over medium heat for 3-4 minutes per side.
3. Add cheddar cheese and let it melt.
4. Toast brioche buns and spread truffle aioli.
5. Place burgers on buns and carefully top with gold leaf before serving.

Caviar and Champagne Risotto

Ingredients:

- 1 cup Arborio rice
- ½ cup champagne
- 3 cups chicken or seafood stock
- 1 tbsp butter
- ¼ cup grated Parmesan cheese
- 2 tbsp crème fraîche
- 1 oz premium caviar

Instructions:

1. In a pan, melt butter and toast the rice for 2 minutes.
2. Add champagne and let it absorb.
3. Slowly add stock, stirring constantly until rice is tender.
4. Stir in Parmesan and crème fraîche.
5. Serve topped with caviar.

Saffron-Infused Seafood Paella

Ingredients:

- 1 cup Arborio or Bomba rice
- 3 cups seafood stock
- ¼ tsp saffron threads
- ½ lb shrimp, cleaned
- ½ lb mussels
- ½ lb calamari rings
- 1 tomato, diced
- ½ onion, chopped
- 2 cloves garlic, minced
- 1 tsp smoked paprika
- 2 tbsp olive oil

Instructions:

1. Heat olive oil in a pan, sauté onions and garlic.
2. Add rice, saffron, paprika, and tomatoes.
3. Slowly add seafood stock, stirring occasionally.
4. When rice is almost done, add shrimp, mussels, and calamari.
5. Cover and cook until seafood is tender and mussels open.

Smoked Duck Breast with Cherry Reduction

Ingredients:

- 2 duck breasts
- ½ cup fresh cherries, pitted
- ¼ cup red wine
- 1 tbsp honey
- ½ tsp salt
- ½ tsp black pepper

Instructions:

1. Score duck breast skin, season with salt and pepper.
2. Sear skin-side down until crispy, then flip and cook to medium-rare.
3. Remove and let rest.
4. Simmer cherries, red wine, and honey until thickened.
5. Slice duck and serve with the cherry reduction.

Hand-Rolled Uni Sushi with Shiso

Ingredients:

- 1 cup sushi rice, cooked
- 4 pieces fresh uni (sea urchin)
- 4 shiso leaves
- 1 tbsp rice vinegar
- 1 tsp sugar
- 1 sheet nori, cut into strips

Instructions:

1. Mix rice vinegar and sugar into warm sushi rice.
2. Place shiso leaf on rice and add a piece of uni.
3. Roll into a sushi hand roll using nori.

Bone Marrow and Truffle Ravioli

Ingredients:

- 1 cup flour
- 1 egg
- 2 tbsp bone marrow, softened
- 1 tbsp black truffle oil
- ¼ cup ricotta cheese
- ½ tsp salt

Instructions:

1. Make pasta dough with flour, egg, and salt. Let rest for 30 minutes.
2. Mix bone marrow, ricotta, and truffle oil for filling.
3. Roll out pasta, cut into squares, and fill with the mixture.
4. Seal edges and boil for 3 minutes. Serve with truffle butter.

A5 Wagyu Tartare with Quail Egg

Ingredients:

- 4 oz A5 Wagyu beef, finely chopped
- 1 quail egg yolk
- ½ tsp Dijon mustard
- ½ tsp soy sauce
- ½ tsp truffle oil
- ¼ tsp salt
- ¼ tsp black pepper

Instructions:

1. Mix chopped Wagyu with mustard, soy sauce, truffle oil, salt, and pepper.
2. Shape into a small round on a plate.
3. Top with a raw quail egg yolk before serving.

Lobster Thermidor with Cognac Sauce

Ingredients:

- 2 lobster tails
- 2 tbsp butter
- 1 shallot, finely chopped
- ¼ cup cognac
- ½ cup heavy cream
- ¼ cup Parmesan cheese, grated
- 1 tbsp Dijon mustard
- ½ tsp paprika
- Salt and pepper to taste
- 2 tbsp breadcrumbs
- 1 tbsp chopped parsley

Instructions:

1. Preheat the oven to 400°F (200°C).
2. Boil lobster tails for 5 minutes, then remove the meat and chop it.
3. In a pan, melt butter and sauté shallots. Add cognac and flambé.
4. Stir in cream, Parmesan, mustard, paprika, salt, and pepper.
5. Add chopped lobster, cook briefly, then spoon the mixture back into shells.
6. Sprinkle breadcrumbs and bake for 10 minutes until golden brown.
7. Garnish with parsley and serve.

Charcoal-Grilled Tomahawk Steak

Ingredients:

- 1 tomahawk steak (about 2.5 lbs)
- 2 tbsp olive oil
- 1 tbsp coarse salt
- 1 tbsp black pepper
- 2 sprigs rosemary
- 3 garlic cloves, smashed

Instructions:

1. Let the steak rest at room temperature for 1 hour.
2. Rub with olive oil, salt, and pepper.
3. Preheat the charcoal grill and sear steak for 3-4 minutes per side.
4. Move to indirect heat and grill for 20-25 minutes to desired doneness.
5. Let rest for 10 minutes before slicing.

Black Truffle and Parmesan Gnocchi

Ingredients:

- 2 large russet potatoes
- 1 cup flour
- 1 egg
- ½ tsp salt
- 2 tbsp black truffle oil
- ¼ cup grated Parmesan cheese

Instructions:

1. Bake potatoes at 400°F (200°C) for 1 hour, then scoop out the flesh.
2. Mash potatoes, mix with flour, egg, and salt.
3. Roll into ropes, cut into 1-inch pieces, and boil until they float.
4. Toss with truffle oil and Parmesan before serving.

Miso-Glazed Black Cod

Ingredients:

- 2 black cod fillets
- ¼ cup white miso paste
- 2 tbsp sake
- 2 tbsp mirin
- 1 tbsp sugar
- 1 tbsp soy sauce

Instructions:

1. Mix miso, sake, mirin, sugar, and soy sauce to make the marinade.
2. Marinate cod for 24 hours in the refrigerator.
3. Preheat the oven to 400°F (200°C) and bake for 12 minutes.
4. Broil for 2-3 minutes until caramelized.

Oxtail Consommé with Wild Mushrooms

Ingredients:

- 2 lbs oxtail
- 1 onion, chopped
- 2 carrots, chopped
- 2 celery stalks, chopped
- 4 cups beef stock
- ½ cup wild mushrooms, sliced
- 1 egg white

Instructions:

1. Roast oxtail at 400°F (200°C) for 30 minutes.
2. Simmer with vegetables in beef stock for 4 hours.
3. Strain, then clarify with egg white to remove impurities.
4. Serve with wild mushrooms.

Szechuan Peppercorn-Crusted Lamb Chops

Ingredients:

- 4 lamb chops
- 1 tbsp Szechuan peppercorns, crushed
- 1 tsp salt
- 1 tbsp soy sauce
- 1 tbsp sesame oil
- 1 garlic clove, minced

Instructions:

1. Mix soy sauce, sesame oil, garlic, and peppercorns.
2. Marinate lamb chops for 2 hours.
3. Sear in a hot pan for 3 minutes per side.
4. Let rest before serving.

48-Hour Braised Short Ribs

Ingredients:

- 4 beef short ribs
- 1 bottle red wine
- 2 cups beef stock
- 1 onion, chopped
- 2 carrots, chopped
- 3 garlic cloves, smashed

Instructions:

1. Sear short ribs in a pan.
2. Place in a slow cooker with wine, stock, and vegetables.
3. Braise at 200°F (95°C) for 48 hours.
4. Strain and reduce sauce before serving.

Peking Duck with Caviar Pancakes

Ingredients:

- 1 whole duck
- 2 tbsp honey
- 1 tbsp soy sauce
- 1 tbsp rice vinegar
- ½ cup caviar
- 10 thin pancakes

Instructions:

1. Blanch duck in boiling water, then dry for 24 hours.
2. Brush with honey, soy sauce, and vinegar.
3. Roast at 375°F (190°C) for 1.5 hours.
4. Serve with pancakes and caviar.

Alaskan King Crab in Garlic Butter Sauce

Ingredients:

- 2 lbs Alaskan king crab legs
- 4 tbsp butter
- 4 garlic cloves, minced
- 1 tbsp lemon juice
- ½ tsp chili flakes

Instructions:

1. Melt butter, sauté garlic, and add lemon juice.
2. Steam crab legs for 5 minutes.
3. Toss crab in garlic butter sauce before serving.

Handmade Burrata with Aged Balsamic

Ingredients:

- 1 cup fresh mozzarella curd
- ½ cup heavy cream
- ½ tsp salt
- 2 tbsp aged balsamic vinegar

Instructions:

1. Heat mozzarella curd until pliable.
2. Fill with heavy cream and salt.
3. Shape into burrata and chill.
4. Drizzle with balsamic before serving.

Black Truffle and Lobster Mac & Cheese

Ingredients:

- 1 lb elbow macaroni
- 2 lobster tails, cooked and chopped
- 2 tbsp butter
- 2 tbsp flour
- 2 cups heavy cream
- 1 cup whole milk
- 1 cup sharp cheddar, shredded
- 1 cup Gruyère cheese, shredded
- 2 tbsp black truffle oil
- ½ cup panko breadcrumbs
- 2 tbsp Parmesan cheese, grated
- Salt and pepper to taste

Instructions:

1. Cook pasta al dente and set aside.
2. In a saucepan, melt butter and whisk in flour.
3. Slowly add cream and milk, stirring until thickened.
4. Stir in cheddar, Gruyère, truffle oil, salt, and pepper.
5. Fold in pasta and lobster, then transfer to a baking dish.
6. Mix panko and Parmesan, sprinkle on top, and bake at 375°F (190°C) for 15 minutes.

Japanese A5 Wagyu Sukiyaki

Ingredients:

- ½ lb A5 Wagyu beef, thinly sliced
- 1 block tofu, cubed
- 1 cup shiitake mushrooms
- 1 cup Napa cabbage, chopped
- ½ cup green onions, sliced
- 2 eggs
- 1 cup dashi
- ½ cup soy sauce
- ¼ cup mirin
- ¼ cup sake
- 1 tbsp sugar

Instructions:

1. Heat a cast iron pan and sear Wagyu briefly. Set aside.
2. Add dashi, soy sauce, mirin, sake, and sugar to the pan.
3. Simmer tofu, mushrooms, cabbage, and green onions in broth.
4. Return Wagyu to the pan, cook briefly, then serve with raw egg for dipping.

Saffron and Champagne Butter Scallops

Ingredients:

- 6 large sea scallops
- 2 tbsp butter
- ¼ cup champagne
- 1 pinch saffron threads
- 1 clove garlic, minced
- Salt and pepper to taste

Instructions:

1. Sear scallops in butter for 2 minutes per side.
2. Remove and deglaze the pan with champagne.
3. Add saffron and garlic, reducing slightly.
4. Return scallops to the pan and coat in sauce.

Dry-Aged Ribeye with Smoked Salt

Ingredients:

- 1 dry-aged ribeye steak (16 oz)
- 1 tbsp olive oil
- 1 tsp smoked salt
- 1 tsp black pepper

Instructions:

1. Preheat a cast iron skillet to high heat.
2. Rub steak with olive oil, smoked salt, and pepper.
3. Sear for 3 minutes per side, then rest for 10 minutes.

Caramelized Miso Chilean Sea Bass

Ingredients:

- 2 Chilean sea bass fillets
- ¼ cup white miso paste
- 2 tbsp mirin
- 1 tbsp soy sauce
- 1 tbsp sugar
- 1 tbsp butter

Instructions:

1. Marinate sea bass in miso, mirin, soy sauce, and sugar overnight.
2. Broil for 10 minutes, basting with butter halfway.

Bluefin Tuna Tataki with Ponzu Foam

Ingredients:

- 8 oz bluefin tuna, sashimi grade
- 1 tbsp sesame oil
- ½ cup ponzu sauce
- ¼ tsp soy lecithin (for foam)
- 1 tbsp chives, chopped

Instructions:

1. Sear tuna in sesame oil for 30 seconds per side, then slice.
2. Blend ponzu with soy lecithin to create foam.
3. Serve tuna with ponzu foam and chives.

Fire-Grilled Iberico Pork Chops

Ingredients:

- 2 Iberico pork chops
- 2 tbsp olive oil
- 1 tbsp smoked paprika
- 1 tsp salt
- 1 tsp black pepper

Instructions:

1. Rub chops with olive oil, paprika, salt, and pepper.
2. Grill over high heat for 4 minutes per side.

Roasted Bone Marrow with Truffle Crostini

Ingredients:

- 2 beef marrow bones, cut lengthwise
- 1 tbsp olive oil
- ½ tsp salt
- ½ tsp black pepper
- 1 baguette, sliced
- 1 tbsp truffle oil

Instructions:

1. Roast marrow bones at 450°F (230°C) for 15 minutes.
2. Brush baguette slices with truffle oil and toast.
3. Scoop marrow onto crostini.

24-Hour Slow-Smoked Brisket

Ingredients:

- 5 lb beef brisket
- 2 tbsp salt
- 2 tbsp black pepper
- 1 tbsp smoked paprika
- 1 tbsp garlic powder
- 1 cup wood chips

Instructions:

1. Rub brisket with spices and let rest overnight.
2. Smoke at 225°F (107°C) for 24 hours using wood chips.
3. Let rest before slicing.

Lobster and Caviar Eggs Benedict

Ingredients:

- 2 English muffins
- 2 poached eggs
- 1 lobster tail, cooked and chopped
- 2 tbsp caviar
- ½ cup hollandaise sauce

Instructions:

1. Toast muffins and top with lobster.
2. Add poached eggs and hollandaise sauce.
3. Garnish with caviar.

Duck Confit with Blackberry Glaze

Ingredients:

- 2 duck legs
- 1 cup duck fat
- 1 tsp salt
- ½ tsp black pepper
- ½ cup blackberries
- 1 tbsp balsamic vinegar

Instructions:

1. Salt duck legs and slow-cook in duck fat at 225°F (107°C) for 3 hours.
2. Sear skin-side down until crisp.
3. Simmer blackberries with balsamic for glaze and drizzle over duck.

Sous Vide Filet Mignon with Bordelaise

Ingredients:

- 2 filet mignon steaks (6 oz each)
- 2 sprigs thyme
- 1 clove garlic, crushed
- 2 tbsp butter
- Salt and black pepper to taste
- 1 cup red wine
- ½ cup beef stock
- 1 shallot, finely chopped
- 1 tbsp butter (for Bordelaise sauce)

Instructions:

1. **Sous Vide the Steak:** Season steaks with salt and pepper, vacuum seal with thyme and garlic, and cook at 130°F (54°C) for 1.5 hours.
2. **Prepare Bordelaise Sauce:** Sauté shallots in butter, add wine and beef stock, and reduce by half. Strain and keep warm.
3. **Sear the Steak:** Sear steaks in a hot pan for 30 seconds per side.
4. **Serve:** Drizzle Bordelaise sauce over steaks.

Foie Gras-Topped Wagyu Burger

Ingredients:

- 2 Wagyu beef patties (8 oz each)
- 2 brioche buns
- 2 slices foie gras
- 1 tbsp butter
- ½ cup caramelized onions
- 2 tbsp fig jam
- Salt and black pepper to taste

Instructions:

1. Season and grill Wagyu patties to desired doneness.
2. Sear foie gras in butter for 30 seconds per side.
3. Assemble burgers with fig jam, caramelized onions, and foie gras.

Wild Mushroom and White Wine Risotto

Ingredients:

- 1 cup Arborio rice
- 2 tbsp butter
- ½ cup dry white wine
- 4 cups chicken stock, heated
- 1 cup mixed wild mushrooms, chopped
- ½ cup Parmesan cheese, grated
- Salt and black pepper to taste

Instructions:

1. Sauté mushrooms in butter, set aside.
2. Toast Arborio rice in butter, deglaze with white wine.
3. Gradually add stock, stirring constantly.
4. Stir in mushrooms and Parmesan before serving.

Périgord Truffle Omelette

Ingredients:

- 3 eggs
- 1 tbsp butter
- 1 tbsp heavy cream
- 1 tbsp Périgord truffle, shaved
- Salt and pepper to taste

Instructions:

1. Whisk eggs with cream, salt, and pepper.
2. Cook gently in butter over low heat, folding softly.
3. Top with shaved truffle.

Honey-Glazed Roasted Poussin

Ingredients:

- 1 whole poussin (young chicken)
- 2 tbsp honey
- 1 tbsp soy sauce
- 1 clove garlic, minced
- 1 tsp fresh thyme
- Salt and pepper to taste

Instructions:

1. Season poussin with salt, pepper, and thyme.
2. Roast at 375°F (190°C) for 30 minutes.
3. Glaze with honey and soy sauce, then broil for 5 minutes.

Braised Venison with Red Wine Reduction

Ingredients:

- 2 venison steaks
- 1 cup red wine
- ½ cup beef stock
- 1 shallot, chopped
- 1 tbsp butter
- 1 sprig rosemary
- Salt and pepper to taste

Instructions:

1. Sear venison steaks, then remove from pan.
2. Sauté shallots, then deglaze with red wine and stock.
3. Simmer steaks in sauce for 1 hour, then stir in butter.

Saffron-Butter Poached Langoustines

Ingredients:

- 6 langoustines, peeled
- ½ cup butter
- 1 pinch saffron
- ½ cup white wine

Instructions:

1. Melt butter with saffron and white wine.
2. Poach langoustines gently for 5 minutes.

Uni Carbonara with Freshly Cracked Pepper

Ingredients:

- 8 oz spaghetti
- 2 egg yolks
- 2 tbsp uni (sea urchin)
- ½ cup Parmesan cheese, grated
- 1 tsp black pepper

Instructions:

1. Cook pasta and mix with egg yolks, uni, and Parmesan.
2. Toss with black pepper and serve.

Blackened Mahi-Mahi with Pineapple Salsa

Ingredients:

- 2 mahi-mahi fillets
- 1 tbsp Cajun seasoning
- ½ cup pineapple, diced
- 1 tbsp lime juice
- 1 tbsp cilantro, chopped

Instructions:

1. Coat mahi-mahi with Cajun seasoning and sear.
2. Serve with pineapple salsa.

Lobster Bisque with Cognac Cream

Ingredients:

- 2 lobster tails
- 2 tbsp butter
- ½ cup Cognac
- 2 cups heavy cream
- 1 cup seafood stock
- 1 shallot, minced

Instructions:

1. Sauté shallots, add lobster shells, then deglaze with Cognac.
2. Simmer with seafood stock, blend, then strain.
3. Stir in cream and lobster meat.

Aged Parmesan and Black Truffle Fondue

Ingredients:

- 2 cups aged Parmesan, grated
- 1 cup Gruyère, grated
- 1 cup dry white wine
- 1 tbsp cornstarch
- 2 tbsp black truffle, finely shaved
- 1 clove garlic, halved
- Freshly ground black pepper to taste
- Assorted bread, vegetables, and charcuterie for dipping

Instructions:

1. Rub the inside of a fondue pot with garlic.
2. Heat wine over medium-low heat.
3. Toss cheese with cornstarch, then gradually add to the wine, stirring until smooth.
4. Stir in black truffle and season with pepper.
5. Serve with dipping items.

Charcoal-Grilled Mediterranean Octopus

Ingredients:

- 1 whole octopus (2-3 lbs), cleaned
- 2 bay leaves
- 4 cloves garlic, smashed
- ½ cup olive oil
- Juice of 1 lemon
- 1 tsp smoked paprika
- 1 tsp sea salt
- ½ tsp black pepper

Instructions:

1. Simmer octopus in water with bay leaves and garlic for 45 minutes.
2. Cool, then cut into tentacles.
3. Toss with olive oil, lemon juice, paprika, salt, and pepper.
4. Char over high heat until slightly crispy.

Porcini-Dusted Veal Chop

Ingredients:

- 2 veal chops (12 oz each)
- 2 tbsp dried porcini mushrooms, ground into powder
- 1 tbsp olive oil
- 1 tbsp butter
- 2 cloves garlic, crushed
- 1 sprig rosemary
- Salt and pepper to taste

Instructions:

1. Rub veal chops with porcini powder, salt, and pepper.
2. Sear in olive oil and butter with garlic and rosemary.
3. Cook to medium-rare (135°F/57°C) and rest before serving.

Yuzu-Marinated Hamachi Crudo

Ingredients:

- 6 oz hamachi (yellowtail), thinly sliced
- 2 tbsp yuzu juice
- 1 tbsp soy sauce
- ½ tsp sesame oil
- 1 tsp jalapeño, thinly sliced
- 1 tsp chives, finely chopped

Instructions:

1. Arrange hamachi slices on a plate.
2. Drizzle with yuzu juice, soy sauce, and sesame oil.
3. Garnish with jalapeño and chives.

Spiced Moroccan Lamb Tagine

Ingredients:

- 2 lbs lamb shoulder, cubed
- 2 tbsp olive oil
- 1 onion, chopped
- 3 cloves garlic, minced
- 1 tsp ground cumin
- 1 tsp ground cinnamon
- 1 tsp smoked paprika
- ½ tsp saffron threads
- 1 cup chickpeas, cooked
- ½ cup dried apricots, chopped
- 1 cup beef broth

Instructions:

1. Brown lamb in olive oil.
2. Sauté onions and garlic, then add spices.
3. Return lamb, add broth, and simmer for 2 hours.
4. Stir in chickpeas and apricots before serving.

24-Hour Slow-Braised Pork Belly

Ingredients:

- 2 lbs pork belly
- ½ cup soy sauce
- ¼ cup mirin
- ¼ cup sake
- 2 tbsp honey
- 4 cloves garlic, minced
- 1-inch ginger, sliced

Instructions:

1. Marinate pork belly overnight in soy sauce, mirin, sake, honey, garlic, and ginger.
2. Slow-braise at 250°F (120°C) for 6 hours.
3. Chill overnight, then sear before serving.

Sea Urchin and Bottarga Pasta

Ingredients:

- 8 oz fresh pasta
- 2 tbsp olive oil
- 1 clove garlic, minced
- ½ cup sea urchin (uni)
- 1 tbsp bottarga, grated
- ½ cup white wine
- 2 tbsp butter

Instructions:

1. Cook pasta and reserve ½ cup pasta water.
2. Sauté garlic in olive oil, add white wine, and reduce.
3. Stir in sea urchin and butter. Toss with pasta and top with bottarga.

Espresso-Rubbed Prime Rib

Ingredients:

- 1 bone-in prime rib (4 lbs)
- 2 tbsp espresso powder
- 1 tbsp sea salt
- 1 tbsp black pepper
- 1 tbsp smoked paprika
- 2 cloves garlic, minced
- 2 tbsp olive oil

Instructions:

1. Rub prime rib with espresso, salt, pepper, paprika, garlic, and olive oil.
2. Roast at 250°F (120°C) for 3 hours, then sear at 500°F (260°C) for 5 minutes.

Miso Caramelized Scallops with Sake Reduction

Ingredients:

- 6 large sea scallops
- 1 tbsp miso paste
- 1 tbsp butter
- ¼ cup sake
- 1 tbsp mirin

Instructions:

1. Sear scallops in butter until golden brown.
2. Deglaze with sake and mirin, then stir in miso.

www.ingramcontent.com/pod-product-compliance
Lightning Source LLC
LaVergne TN
LVHW081501060526
838201LV00056BA/2867